PRAISE FOR
WINNERS AND LOSERS

"Don Schmincke is one of the most sophisticated thinkers I've ever met, and he's led one of the most interesting lives I've ever heard about (Think Peter Drucker meets Indiana Jones). His book, *Winners and Losers*, may turn your world upside down. He teaches you not just how to win in business, but how to use losing as a way of making your wins grow even bigger."
—Mark Levy, founder of Levy Innovation and creator of the business concept Your Big Sexy Idea®

"This groundbreaking book uncovers controversial insights from anthropology, evolutionary psychology, and personal experimentation. Prepare for 200% to 300% improvements in sales, profits, and organizational performance, backed by real-world success stories. Say goodbye to quick-fix solutions and embrace a paradigm shift in your thinking. With Don's unconventional wisdom, you'll debunk myths, learn from failures, and tap into the power of your biology for entrepreneurial success. Buckle up for an extraordinary ride that will transform the way you approach business!"
—Joel G. Block, Advantage Player™, keynote speaker, hedge fund manager, and venture capitalist

"Unleash your entrepreneurial genius with *Winners and Losers*, by Don Schmincke."
—Dov Baron, *Inc. Magazine* Top 100 Leadership Speaker, Top 30 Global Leadership Guru, creator of *Inc. Magazine* #1 Podcast for Fortune 500 Executives

If this is not the bottom, then how deep does this pit go?

This was the question of a distraught parent whose child is daily indoctrinated in the socially left curriculum of a New York public school. Although the school system claims that it is bankrupt, it did find enough money to publish a new curriculum that teaches the acceptance of homosexuality in the first grade and mutual masturbation in junior high. "Condoms," say some parents, "are given to the students instead of textbooks; and classes in how to practice various forms of immorality have become a substitute for the three R's."

Little wonder former education secretary William J. Bennet gives our nation a failing grade. In his *Leading Cultural Indicators* research, he has shown that during the past thirty years there has been

- a 560 percent increase in violent crime
- more than a 400 percent increase in illegitimate births
- a quadrupling in divorce rates
- a tripling of the percentage of children living in single parent homes
- more than a 200 percent increase in the teenage suicide rate
- and a drop of almost 80 points in SAT scores

No matter how much the government spends on pathologies, he says, the situation is only becoming worse: "Many of the most serious social and behavioral problems we now face (particularly among our young) are remarkably resistant to government cures."

Never before have our children been less cared for, less emotionally healthy, and less prepared for life. When novelist Walter Percy was asked what concerned him most about the future of our nation, he said, "Probably the fear of seeing America, with all of its great strength, beauty and freedom . . . gradually subside into decay through default and be defeated, not by the Communist movement, demonstrably a bankrupt system, but from within by weariness, boredom, cynicism, greed and in the end *helplessness before its great problems*."

Helplessness before its great problems! Resistant to government cures! When a Chicago newspaper asked its readers for suggestions on how to stop the alarming crime rate in the inner city, the response (even from church leaders) was largely silence. How ironic that our nation with its mighty resources is unable to restore respect for human life, commitment in marriage, and care for children. Even secularists are

4

beginning to realize that our problems are not educational, not cultural, and not even moral, but spiritual. *We have lost our way.*

If we could speak to our "Founding Fathers," they would tell us simply, "You have forgotten God." Historians can debate the details of what each of them believed, but all of them firmly agreed that faith in God was the foundation of democracy. Respect and decency cannot be maintained apart from a belief in God and moral absolutes. As the saying goes, when men cease believing in God they do not believe in nothing; rather, *they believe in anything.*

Will America be given another chance? Will God again be honored in our homes, schools, and courts? Do we have reason to believe that "In God We Trust" will be more than an anachronism still engraved on our coins but not on our hearts? Can we win the battle for America's heart and soul?

Thankfully, there are tens of thousands of Christians who are swimming against our cultural stream, refusing to be intimidated by social pressures, the agenda of the media, and the world's seductive values of wealth and pleasure. When sounding the alarm, it is easy for us to fall into the "Elijah syndrome," who in a moment of skewed perspective cried out, "I have been very zealous for the Lord the God of hosts . . . And I alone am left; and they seek my life to take it away" (1 Kings 19:14).

He thought the whole nation had collapsed into paganism! But to this doom-and-gloom prophet, the Lord gave this startling reply: "Yet I will leave 7,000 in Israel, all the knees that have not bowed to Baal and every mouth that has not kissed him" (v. 18).

As we shall see later, not all news about America is bad. There are many Elijahs who are sounding the trumpet. But we must also candidly admit that no country has had more Christian radio stations, more books, more seminars, and more churches with proportionately less impact on society. If, as Elton Trueblood has said, the strength of the church should be determined by its impact on its surrounding culture, we desperately need an injection of spiritual life. We are confounded with the pollsters who tell us that religion is up but morality is down.

Ideally, we could win our cultural war through the positive impact of individual Christians living out their faith wherever God has planted them. Some think there are faint signs that the nation is moving away from the socially left policies of our educators, entertainers, judges, and politicians. Perhaps there will be a renewed appreciation for family values, a respect for human life, and a gradual restoration of our religious freedoms. Thanks to the faithfulness of believers, even reverence for God might make a comeback.

Though such a scenario is possible, it would not address the deeper issues that are so important to us as Christians. We cannot be satisfied with political, judicial, or even moral transformation. Our nation needs to hear a message that will actually change the human heart. We need a renewal that can only be effected by widespread repentance before the Almighty whom we have so grievously offended. The forces of evil are so deeply entrenched that any cultural shifts will only be cosmetic unless they are accompanied by a spiritual awakening that affects large segments of our population.

There is reason to believe that only a national revival can pull us out of the ditch into which we have slid. I am convinced — as all of us must be — that every human resource is now inadequate and only the direct intervention of God can reverse our spiritual direction. If America will really be given another chance, at least some kingdoms of darkness will have to fall like dominoes. That can only happen if God chooses to show us the mercy we most assuredly do not deserve. It can only happen if the gospel of the New Testament is preached and believed.

This booklet is written to raise our sights, to increase our faith in the possibility of a national revival. We must restudy the Bible and see what God has done in the history of the church. *We must believe God for something more than our generation has seen.*

The purpose of this booklet is fourfold:

1. To survey America's three Great Awakenings to learn what we can from God's gracious work in our past

2. To learn to recognize a revival by observing the first "Great Awakening" in the history of the church

3. To compare our culture with that of the past to better understand the demands that a national revival might require from the believing church

4. To learn what we can do to maximize our spiritual potential and prepare for whatever God might yet choose to do in this great nation

America has had several periods of revival. During three of these occasions there has been a widespread restoration of the people of God that resulted in tens of thousands of conversions. We have important lessons to learn from these unusual epochs of blessing. Carefully read these historical sketches and ask the question, *What would happen if God were to do it again?*

THE FIRST GREAT AWAKENING
(1740–43)

The spiritual history of a nation goes in cycles. The convictions of one generation are often diminished in the next; then God begins the process of renewal. When the Puritans came to the United States, they brought with them a well-defined doctrinal and moral standard. Their devotion to God is legendary. Yet, for all that, by the end of the 1600s, decline had set in and moral decay threatened the purity of the church.

In 1679 a "reforming synod" was called to delineate the faults of the church. Some of the indictments included the following: (1) spiritual pride; (2) neglect of church and ordinances; (3) backbiting and division; (4) worldliness, profanity, and so on; (5) drunkenness and selfishness; (6) a lack of concern for the welfare of others; and (7) unbelief. There was not only concern about individual apathy but about the corporate deadness of the churches. Reforms were instituted that did little to curb the decline.

Then God sent special men into this

cultural decay to stir up the Christians and to confront the unsaved with the gospel. Solomon Stoddard, a pastor at Northampton, Massachusetts, was a soul-winner whom God blessed with "five harvests," as he called them, special times of spiritual refreshing when many were converted and new spiritual life sprung up within the community. He challenged his congregation to believe God for continual "harvests."

The second, and possibly the most famous, of the New England revivalists was Stoddard's grandson, Jonathan Edwards. After studying at Yale he became the assistant to his grandfather in Northampton, and when his grandfather died two years later the young theologian had the responsibility of leading this congregation. His disciplined study and keen mind made him America's greatest theologian.

In 1734 the Holy Spirit worked mightily in Edwards's congregation and three hundred souls were saved. Edwards, who understood the concept of "harvests" from his grandfather, recognized this as a mighty work of God that could inspire others toward revival. He published a booklet entitled *A Faithful Narrative of the Surprising Work of God.* "God," he said, "poured contempt on all that human strength, wisdom, prudence, and sufficiency, which men have been wont to trust . . . so as to greatly cross, rebuke, and chastise the pride and the other corruptions of men." Through this book revival spread to other churches and even across the ocean to England.

Edwards preached his sermon, "Sinners in the Hands of an Angry God," not to frighten his hearers but to rationally persuade them to flee to Christ for forgiveness and protection from God's wrath. One observer recorded, "So vivid and solemn was the impression made that [we supposed] that as soon as Mr. Edwards should close his discourse, the Judge would descend and the final separation take place." During Edwards's sermons people would cry out in conviction and repentance. Others wept softly, mourning over their sins.

George Whitefield was the third and most popular leader of this revival movement. He was born in a tavern in England in 1714, and his father died when George was two years of age. At the age of fifteen he had to drop out of school and help his mother in the tavern for eighteen months. Later he attended Oxford and joined the Holy Club, where he met John and Charles Wesley.

After weeks of spiritual anguish seeking salvation and freedom from "proud hellish thoughts," Whitefield discovered the gospel as the true ground of the sinner's justification. "I found and felt in myself that I was delivered from the burden that had so heavily oppressed. The spirit of mourning was taken from me and I knew what it was to rejoice in God my Savior."

He was ordained in 1736 when only twenty-two years of age! Even then, thousands came to hear him preach, often to criticize. Nevertheless, hundreds left inspired, convicted, and converted. His instant popularity was a phenomenon that probably has not been repeated in history. When he came to the United States, he and Jonathan Edwards became close friends. "Edwards lit the fuse but Whitefield fanned it into a flame" historians tell us. These two revivalists preached to large crowds and witnessed thousands of conversions.

In 1739 Whitefield made a second trip to the United States and had remarkable success in Philadelphia, where he met a lifelong friend, Benjamin Franklin. Franklin wrote of the revival, "From being thoughtless and indifferent about religion it seem'd as if all the world were growing religious, that one could not walk through the town in an evening without hearing psalms sung in different families of every street."

How might this revival be described? "Revival" said one observer, "broke upon the slumbering churches like a thunderbolt rushing out of a clear sky." God breathed new life into the apathetic churches, and whole communities were affected.

The revival was preceded by organized, united prayer. In 1743, Edwards, who believed that corporate prayer was more effective than the accumulated prayers of individuals, encouraged "concerts of prayer" and suggested days for prayer and fasting. Churches in other colonies followed suit. Then the prayer movement spread to Scotland and England.

Conviction of sin was overwhelming and geographically widespread. Some said they saw hell open before them with themselves ready to fall into it. There was a seriousness, an understanding that each man lived in the presence of a holy and awesome God. There was no attempt to get people saved until they were thoroughly convinced they were lost!

The crowds listened to Whitefield with breathless silence broken only by sobs. When miners crowded to hear him, one reported, "The tears made white furrows down their smutty cheeks.... Mechanics shut up their shops, and the day laborers throw down their tools to go and hear him preach, and few return unaffected."

Whitefield often wept when he preached, asserting that he was weeping for those who would not weep for themselves. His deep personal conviction left people with a great sense of repentance and spiritual expectancy. "His heart," it was said, was "aglow with love as he poured out a torrent of eloquence which was almost irresistible." He preached as if there were no tomorrow.

Finally, there was a return to righteousness. One observer claims that it would have been possible to leave a bag of gold on the street and it would not be stolen! Taverns were closed, families were reconciled, and young people became sober in their pursuit of God. Estimates regarding the number of conversions vary, but at least 50,000 were believed to be converted, greatly affecting the culture of the day.

The skeptics said the revival was nothing but an emotional phenomenon. In the compelling book titled *Religious Affections*, Edwards defended what God had done. He showed from Scripture how to distinguish between the false and the true spiritual experiences. Whenever God works in an extraordinary way, Satan comes to imitate and confuse, but this does not diminish

God's work. *If we pray for rain,* someone has said, *let us not complain about the mud!*

During the First Great Awakening, all of society was dramatically affected. Through the work of the Wesleys in England and the revival movement in the United States, much of the English speaking world returned to its Christian roots. Colleges such as Dartmouth and Princeton were training grounds for ministers of the Christian faith. God had blessed His people with a bountiful "harvest," and they were grateful.

Let us learn this lesson well: *A genuine spiritual revival can do more to transform culture than all of our political/social activism.* Perhaps the reason we have had so little impact on society despite all of our efforts is that *we as evangelicals have lost our confidence in the power of the gospel to save sinners — yes, even great sinners.*

Culture can change only when people change; people can be changed only by Christ. Do we still believe this?

THE SECOND GREAT AWAKENING (1790–1860)

By 1800 a million people had made their way west to states such as Kentucky, Louisiana, and Tennessee. But along with this migration, there was an accompanying disinterest in religion. In the East the church had given society stability, but as the population moved west the power of religion over the minds of men faded. There was immorality, alcoholism, and unbelief.

Then God began to demonstrate His power. Under the leadership of James Mc-Gready (1762–1817) a spiritual awakening began at a camp meeting in Kentucky. The power of God seemed to shake the whole assembly. One observer says that the cries of the distressed arose almost as loud as the preacher's voice. No person seemed to want to go home; hunger and sleep appeared to affect no one; eternal things were the vast concern.

A similar but larger camp meeting was organized by Barton Stone (1772–1844), a Presbyterian pastor at Cain Ridge. Between 10,000 and 25,000 came with wagons, carriages, and by foot. People fell down, crying out, trembling, and not infrequently "sinners dropping down on every hand, shrieking, groaning, crying for mercy, convulsed; professors praying, agonizing, fainting, falling down in distress, for sinners or in raptures of joy!"

Some of these extremes were often used by critics to discredit the meetings. However, undeniably God was at work.

Thanks to circuit riders the whole state of Kentucky was radically affected, and the revival "confounded infidelity and brought untold numbers to the faith."

Meanwhile, in the East, Timothy Dwight, the grandson of Jonathan Edwards, became president of Yale in 1795. The few Christians at the college were so embarrassed about their faith that in order to remain "politically correct" they communicated to one another with a secret code so that they would not be identified!

Dwight decided to confront the infidelity directly by giving a series of lectures on the topic: *Is the Bible the Word of God?* Approximately one-third of the student body (75 out of 225) was converted. During their vacation, they told others about what God had done, and this sparked widespread interest in revival. As the reports spread, a series of revivals took place on other college campuses such as Princeton and Dartmouth.

A similar revival took place at Williams College where in August of 1806 five students, en route to a prayer meeting, took refuge under a haystack during a thunderstorm. While the lightning flashed and the thunder roared, they prayed, committing themselves to worldwide missionary service. Present was Samuel Mills whom God would use to begin a missionary movement that would eventually impact the globe. When revival comes, it spreads!

Charles G. Finney was America's greatest revivalist during the Second Great Awakening. One afternoon he went into the woods, knelt by a log, wrestled with God in prayer, and was converted. In his words, "an overwhelming sense of my wickedness . . . took such powerful possession of me that I cried at the top of my voice and exclaimed that I would not leave that place if all the men on earth and all the devils in Hell surrounded me." Finally, he yielded to God and was overtaken by what he described as waves of "liquid love." He had no doubt he had been soundly converted.

Finney left law and became a revivalist. He exuded such charisma that it was affirmed that when he said the word "Hell" people smelled smoke! The peak of his successful evangelistic efforts was in Rochester, New York, in 1830–31. The whole city was involved as shopkeepers closed down their businesses and taverns shut their doors. The Holy Spirit brought such deep conviction that it was common to see people lying on the ground crying to God for relief from the conviction of the Spirit. Such fear of God spread to other cities in New York and throughout the United States.

Finney was severely criticized because he gave public invitations, allowed women to pray in public, and rejected Calvinism, with its emphasis on predestination and the sovereignty of God. Disillusioned because of those who professed faith and yet gave no evidence of it, he later fell into the error of perfectionism, teaching that only those who attain sinlessness are truly saved.

His enduring legacy is found in his challenging book *Lectures On Revival.* He defined revival as "the renewal of the first love of Christians, resulting in the awakening and conversion of sinners to God." He believed that backsliders had to be brought to repentance and then they would have a desire to see the wicked converted. The power of the world must be broken in their lives and fervent love renewed.

Just as firemen must awaken to fight a fire in the city, so the church must awaken to quench the fires of hell. Christians should be grieved by the wickedness of the wicked. They must weep day and night instead of scolding and reproaching them. Through repentance, prayer, and hard work, a revival can be guaranteed.

The Second Great Awakening reminds

us that God uses people of diverse theological persuasions. Jonathan Edwards and Whitefield were strong Calvinists, believing that a revival could come only by the good pleasure of God. Finney was an Arminian, preaching that people have it within their power alone to either accept or reject Christ and that a revival could be had whenever we want one. "A revival," he said, "is nothing more than the right use of the right means."

By some estimates a million people were converted through the various revival efforts that composed the Second Great Awakening. New spiritual life had been infused into our nation when God sent this series of special "harvests."

What God did in our past should bring hope for our future.

THE THIRD GREAT AWAKENING
(1857–1859)

During the summer of 1857, Jeremiah Calvin Lanphier walked the streets of New York City asking God to show him how to reach the businessmen on Wall Street. He decided to distribute a handbill in offices and warehouses inviting others to come to a noonday prayer meeting. On it were these words:

How often shall I pray? As often as the language of prayer is in my heart; as often as I see my need of help; as often as I feel the power of temptation; as often as I am made sensible of any spiritual declension or feel the aggression of a worldly spirit. In prayer we leave the business of time for that of eternity, and fellowship with men for fellowship with God.

At noon on September, 23, 1857, the door was opened in the meeting hall, but nobody appeared. At 12:30, however, a step on the stairs was heard and another and another; in all, six men gathered to pray. Week by week the crowds grew.

The very next month, October 1857, the stock market crashed and people felt a greater need to seek God. Within six months, a total of 10,000 men were gathering daily for prayer in many places throughout New York City. When the churches were packed, the prayer meetings were moved to theaters.

The *New York Herald* of March 6, 1858, said, "Satan is busy all the morning in Wall Street among the brokers, and all the afternoon and evening the churches are crowded with saints who gambled in the morning."

News about revival spread the revival. One observer noted that whether willingly or unwillingly "the press proclaims God's wonders everywhere." For example, in Albany, New York, an early morning prayer meeting was initiated by state legislators who began with six participants in the room of the Court of Appeals, but soon afterwards all the rooms were overflowing for prayer.

Californians heard of the revival via newspapers, letters, and those who had the good fortune to travel across America bearing good news. Prayer meetings came to Sacramento and San Jose. The daily prayer meetings in the San Francisco area continued with unabated interest and many converts. Word of this revival also reached Great Britain and as far away as India.

Consider the impact of the revival here in Chicago. On March 25, 1858, the *Tribune* reported:

> The noon prayer meeting at Metropolitan Hall yesterday was the largest and most interesting that has yet been held. The body of the house and the gallery were filled considerably before 12:00; and at the time for commencing the exercises the platform, stairways, aisles and entries were all occupied by persons stand-

ing up. During the whole hour, the stairs leading down to the street were filled with persons arriving or retiring unable to gain admittance.

John Wentworth, the mayor of Chicago at the time, stood near the rear end of the hall and listened with great attention to all that was said. Later he commented, "The effects of the present religious movement are to be felt in every phase of society."

The *Chicago Daily Journal* of March 20,1858, reported that the revival was universal and " not limited to a single city or even state, but has spread like fire in every direction. . . . Such an outpouring of religion has not been seen before since the days of Edwards."

In 1856 Dwight L. Moody arrived in Chicago, just two years before the revival came there. One of his biographers says that it was this third awakening that "tossed Moody out of his complacency." Because of his burden for the children of the city, he rented four pews in the Plymouth Church and filled them with his "friends." He wrote home to his mother, "There is a great revival of religion in this city. I go to meeting every night, oh how I enjoy it! It seems as if God was here Himself — Oh mother, pray for us — pray that this will go on until every knee is bowed."

This revival was silent and orderly and did not have the excesses of some the previous revival movements. It was dubbed the "businessman's awakening" because it had no great leaders, no famous revivalists who embodied the movement. Pastors took turns leading the prayer meetings, but no one person or persons dominated. Lay people gave testimonies and helped lead the meetings. Also, it was spread by word of mouth — the fact that God was working in one city was proof that He could do the same in another. It was primarily a revival of prayer. The historian J. Edwin Orr wrote:

> The influence of the awakening was felt everywhere in the nation. It first captured the great cities, but it also spread through every town and village and country hamlet. It swamped schools and colleges. It affected all classes without respect to condition. There was no fanaticism. There was a remarkable unanimity of approval among religious and secular observers alike, with scarcely a critical voice heard anywhere. It seemed to many that the fruits of Pentecost had been repeated.

This revival of prayer had a great impact on the heart of our nation. Hundreds of thousands of people were converted during the period of a few years.

Sometimes God uses highly visible leaders; at other times He simply needs a humble servant of God to begin a prayer meeting. One act of faithfulness can be the spark that ignites a prayer movement that sweeps a nation and other parts of the world.

If America is to be renewed, Christian laymen will be the catalyst to spread the power of revival. Of course, ministers will lead by preaching and praying, but the laity are on the front lines of America's cultural war. *Revival brings boldness, a willingness to witness with joy, not shame.*

A PICTURE OF REVIVAL

Sometimes a revival affects only one church, one college or one community. At other times it spreads, encompassing a wide geographical area. But all revivals have certain characteristics.

How would we recognize a revival if one were to come to the United States? The best description comes to us from the days of Pentecost. When the Holy Spirit came, the early church was given a "jump start" that eventually resonated throughout the world. In fact, on that eventful day the apostles even spoke in other languages, a miracle intended to teach the Jews that the gospel was also intended for the Gentiles. The wonderful works of God would now go to the ends of the earth!

First, there is always *a strong awareness of the presence of God*. Suddenly large numbers of people become conscious that God is among them; personal concerns that are top priority in ordinary life evaporate in what might be called the "manifest presence of God." The people in Jerusalem knew that God was among them, "and great fear came upon the whole church, and upon all who heard these things" (Acts 5:11). During the Great Awakenings, it is said that when ships came to America sailors experienced conviction of sin even before the vessel docked. Those who entered the geographical area of the revival became aware of the presence of God.

Second, *there is opposition*. "And as they were speaking to the people the priests and the captain of the temple guard and the Sadducees came upon them, being greatly disturbed because they were teaching the people and proclaiming in Jesus the resurrection from the dead. And they laid hands on them and put them in jail until the next day for it was already evening (Acts 4:1–3).

The gospel is always a threat to a culture —even religious culture. Some of the greatest enemies of the gospel are within "Christendom."

Make no mistake, if a revival came to the United States it would be strongly opposed not merely by the people of the world but by large segments of the religious establishment. Dead, slumbering churches would awake to resist the work of God. A revival always divides a community; as its influence grows there is little room for neutral ground.

Third, although a revival divides a community it always *unites the true believers* who see in the movement the finger of God. "And when they had been released, they went to their own companions and reported all that the chief priests and elders had to say to them. And when they heard this they lifted up their voices to God with one accord" (Acts 4:23–24). Here was a prayer meeting wholly united in faith and worship.

How long has it been since we have prayed "with one accord"? Revival unites true believers despite their denominational labels and form of worship. The glory of the Lord is more important than any one church or leader.

In a Canadian church two brothers who had not spoken to each other for several years were brought into the basement of the church and encircled by deacons who did not stop praying until the two were reconciled. Both men began to weep as they asked one another for forgiveness. The next evening they sang a duet as a testimony to their reconciliation. This impacted the church, the church impacted its community, and soon a revival spread to many parts of the land.

Revival reconciles husbands to their wives; children are reconciled to their parents and pastors are united to one another. Self-will and "turfism," which divide us, is seen as the sin it truly is.

Yes, divisions are sometimes necessary for theological reasons, but too often we are divided because of personalities, philosophy of ministry, and petty grievances. What lies at the heart of such division are the twin sins of pride and control. When the Holy Spirit shows our sin we are brought to our knees in confession and reconciliation.

Fourth, there is *generosity*. "For there was not a needy person among them, for all who were owners of land or houses would sell them and bring the proceeds of the sales and lay them at the apostles' feet and they would be distributed to each as any had need" (Acts 4:34–35). Too often we are long on sympathy but short on sacrifice. Revival brings a spontaneous outpouring of financial resources because Christians now honestly believe their future is in the hands of God and not in their bank accounts. We know that we are not presently having a revival in America because there are so many unmet financial needs even though our resources are great. During revival people actually look for others they can help.

Fifth, there is *purity*. When Ananias and Sapphira left the impression that they gave the entire price of their land to the church, they were smitten down by God (Acts 5:1–5). God made a powerful statement: We can never be all that we can be if we are dishonest in the presence of our friends — and, most of all, dishonest in the presence of God. Our hypocrisy before men is actually dishonesty before God.

When revival comes, the customs officials will be surprised by people coming to confess that they brought goods into this country illegally; contractors who built houses with inferior materials will rectify such deceptions no matter the personal cost, and the IRS will receive unexpected checks because of past fraud. All such sins are now seen as trivial *because we have not yet seen God.* When a spirit of conviction sweeps a community, the church is purged.

When Ephesus experienced revival, the people brought their occult books and artifacts, and publicly burned them (Acts 19:18–19). What bonfires of pornography, rock music, artifacts, and books of occultism we would have if God's presence was "manifestly felt"!

Finally, there is *evangelism.* As persecution began to build, many people were forced to leave Jerusalem. But they did not remain silent about their faith. "Therefore those who had been scattered went about preaching the Word" (Acts 8:4). When the Spirit has His way, the tongues of the timid are untied, the fearful are given boldness, and the pessimistic are filled with joy. Witnessing becomes a way of life.

When we are revived in God's presence, we will have enough spiritual resources for ourselves and for those around us. We will experience the promise of Christ, "From his innermost being shall flow rivers of living water" (Acts 7:38). We will no longer feel like a cup that is half-full, trying desperately to spill over!

If we should have a national revival, the church would clash with our culture not merely over abortion, homosexuality, and freedom of speech, important as those issues are. *The focus of the debate would be the gospel of Christ.* Those who oppose the revival would mount opposition, but the movement would spread. How helpless evil men would feel if multitudes turned to God!

IS REVIVAL YET POSSIBLE?

Can God do it again? At first blush the answer is *yes*; of course revival is possible as long as God is God. So let's dream for a while: Catch the vision of crowded churches from coast to coast, shops closing during the noon hours for special prayer, and our legislators turning to God for wisdom in making decisions. Think of the nightly news telling the story of tens of thousands of believers making restitution for past wrongs. And reports of thousands of conversions to Christ.

Imagine a country where abortion would become rare, not just through legislation but because mothers valued their children and immorality was on the decline. Imagine a country in which homosexuals repented and sought God for help in overcoming their lifestyles rather than imposing their values on society. Imagine a country where the courts would reflect America's Christian roots.

31

But profound changes have taken place in America since the days of the Great Awakenings. We are not the people we used to be. Revival would be different now than revival was back then.

First, *our culture has changed.* The Great Awakenings took place in an era when there was yet widespread respect for God and the Bible. This was an era in which our legislators could seek God without being sued by the ACLU for disregarding the "separation of church and state." This was the era in which it was possible to pray to God in the public schools and teach moral decency without being hounded by social planners intent on catering to the lowest common moral denominator. This was an era when tolerance for deviancy had not yet become a national icon.

Marital fidelity was respected; pornography, if it existed at all, had to be obtained illegally. There were no Hollywood movies, no violence seen on television, and no psychedelic drugs that twisted the minds of our young people. Abortion was considered to be murder, and family values were respected rather than ridiculed. God, if He was not always worshiped, was at least remembered with respect.

In other words, the three Great Awakenings took place in a cultural context that was, at least in principle, open to the possibility of spiritual life and values. There was a religious foundation that gave stability to society; *guilt* was not yet a dirty word.

Second, our *churches have changed.* By and large the church during those periods of awakening had a perception of God that was remarkably different from that which is now taught from our pulpits (yes, even evangelical pulpits). If Jonathan Edwards were alive today and preached his sermon *"Sinners in the Hands of an Angry God,"* he would not simply be ridiculed by the secularists; many Bible-believing Christians would be profoundly embarrassed. Yet it was the emphasis on God's holiness and justice that brought such deep conviction. As I write, there is a debate within the evangelical camp as to whether we should believe in an eternal hell. Yet even many who argue that hell is eternal would never preach it from the pulpit.

Walk through a bookstore and see what the Christian public is absorbed by — cartloads of self-help books that focus on the human psyche. And while this may not be wrong (many people do need emotional healing in this day of the fractured family), my concern is that these books are read to the exclusion of excellent material on the great doctrinal and book studies of the Bible. A leader in a large Christian publishing company told me candidly that anything that appears to be based on a book of the Bible simply will not sell, no matter how good it is. We cannot have a *spiritual* recovery without a *doctrinal* recovery.

A recent poll suggests that belief in God is widespread. But the word *God* now means many different things to different people. A new America has arisen that knows not the God and Father of our Lord Jesus Christ but has substituted other man-made gods defined according to personal taste and preference. These are tame gods who are as tolerant and nonjudgmental as a contemporary TV talk show host.

Even we as evangelicals have defined God according to our own liking. Is the God in whom our generation has come to trust — our cosmic therapist — even capable of sending a national revival? Do we even know enough about God and His ways so that we know how to pray for the spiritual awakening He might send? Are our thoughts about God so grand, our vision of Him so clear, that we can believe He can save us even at this late hour? Unfortunately *we have been taught to seek God's hand but not God's face.*

Third, I believe that *our concept of revival has changed.* Many Christians would welcome an outpouring of God's Spirit because they think it would restore their personal peace, affluence, and spiritual comfort. To the mind of some, our capitalistic way of life needs spiritual support. We want a revival so that we will not have to trust God in ways that are unfamiliar to us. Even our prayers for an awakening can be self-serving.

Revival, some think, would be the quick fix. No need to fight for moral sanity in the public schools, no need to stand up against gay rights ordinances that threaten the freedom of parents and churches; no need to fight abortion and best of all, no need to reach out to the poverty and crime of our inner cities. When our nation turns to God, we can again maintain our standard of living without the unwelcome prospect of fighting in our present bitter cultural war.

But revival, if it is worth the name, never makes life easier for the church. In 2,000 years of church history God has never bypassed the birth pangs that come to His people when multitudes are born into His kingdom. Every revival stretches the church's comfort zone and brings controversies about doctrine and practice. What is more, a revived church always elicits hostility from an angry world. If a revival were to come, life as a Christian might not be easier but even more difficult.

During a more recent revival movement in Canada in the early 1970s one person said, "Many Christians who prayed for revival rejected it when it came . . . they thought God would smite drug pushers, prostitutes and pornographers with conviction while they walked down the streets. . . . These Christians did not know that God would deal so severely *with them*."

Only God knows the severity of our own discipline if He were to send a national revival. Think of all that we and our churches would have to repent of if a spirit of holiness began to captivate us. We would soon turn from our own aches and pains to focus on the exalted name of God. We would no longer feel sorry for ourselves but would be grieved that God's honor is tramped into the mud through the television we watch, the movies our children attend, and the sinful compromises we've all condoned. God's honor would be our consuming passion.

Of course, God can overcome these barriers and send us a national revival. But we must have a better understanding of what He might require of us should the revival come. God usually waters the earth with intermittent rain, but sometimes He sends a downpour that takes some of the landscape with it. Are we prepared for the uncomfortable challenges renewal would bring? Are we willing to let God do something in our churches that is not listed in the bulletin?

Revival may be America's only answer, but it is not a painless answer. God wounds before He heals; He smites down before He raises up. During revival the tongues of the timid become untied; the pockets of the greedy are opened; the minds of the impure are made clean; the angry ask forgiveness of those they have hurt, and the proud are brought low.

Ask those who have experienced a mighty movement of God and they will tell you it was bittersweet. Imagine your congregation and mine—or better, imagine your life and mine — open before God, and possibly others too. We would not be exempt when the Almighty begins to expose the sins of His people. We may glibly proclaim that we want this nation to have another chance to recapture the meaning of "In God We Trust." But if we knew what such a transformation would personally demand, we just might prefer to leave things as they are. We may have become too comfortable to pay the price.

IS REVIVAL TO BE EXPECTED?

I do not believe that the Bible predicts a worldwide revival before Christ returns (in which America would participate). Yes, someday "all the ends of the earth will remember and turn to the Lord. And all the families of the nations will worship before Thee" (Psalm 22:27). But those of us who hold to what is known as premillennialism (that Christ will return and then establish His kingdom on the earth for a thousand years) believe that these promises await that glorious day. During Christ's personal reign, the nations shall beat their swords into plowshares and their spears into pruning hooks. This revival is not promised for the church age.

On the day of Pentecost Peter quoted Joel 2:28–32, which affirms that the Holy Spirit will be poured out upon all mankind. But the same quotation also says there will be "wonders in the sky above," and "the sun shall be turned to darkness and the moon into blood" (Acts 2:20). Peter quoted Joel because the Holy Spirit was "poured out" at Pentecost, but the complete fulfillment of this prophecy awaits the time of Christ's return.

38

Can we, however, have a revival if we meet the conditions? Second Chronicles 7:14 reads, "If . . . my people who are called by My name humble themselves and pray, and seek My face and turn from their wicked ways, then I will hear from heaven, will forgive their sins and will heal their land." This promise, however, is given to Israel in the land of Canaan. The healing of the land refers to good crops as the preceding verse shows (v. 13).

Yet, in principle this passage can be applied to us. Humility, prayer, and repentance always precede blessing. But this is not a guarantee that our entire nation will be spiritually revived even if God's people meet these conditions. God does not owe us a revival.

Indirect proof that this passage is no guarantee that an entire nation will embrace Christ if believers meet these conditions comes from the pages of church history. The early, persecuted believers in the Roman Empire humbled themselves, turned from their wicked ways, but nevertheless were thrown to lions. Such persecutions continued intermittently for 250 years. The church in Russia humbled itself and prayed for seventy years before it received freedom to worship; yet even now the nation is experiencing economic and spiritual convulsions.

Think of Romania and China, where the church experienced growth and renewal, but the political powers remained firm in their persecution. A spirit of repentance revives believers and strengthens the church, but that does not mean that political and social opposition will end. In other words, a revived church does not guarantee a revived nation.

But God does graciously send periodic "harvests" to His people, and when that happens many are converted in spite of official opposition. Edwards argued that God grants light when the darkness is the greatest and that the history of redemption is driven by revivals. The advance of the church is never a smooth path but follows periods of decline with vigorous times of acceleration. Sometimes those periods of refreshing are confined to a church or area; at other times they affect a nation.

Christ told Nicodemus, "The wind blows where it wishes." We cannot predict the place and extent of the work of the Holy Spirit. We must be ready for the difficult days that may lie ahead — days of revival or days of persecution. Yet, who knows what grace God might yet give us even at this late hour?

Our responsibility is to "set our sails to catch the breeze."

SURVIVAL THROUGH REVIVAL

Our need is overwhelming—What do we do?

Although the word *revival* as used in this booklet refers to a widespread renewal of the church, it always begins with individuals who are "revived." And if one individual can be revived, two can be; and if two then five and if five then ten. Our responsibility is to seek God for ourselves and trust Him for the consequences. If the church is spiritually ill, it is not the fault of the Great Physician.

The question is not whether my country or even my church can be revived if we meet the conditions. The question is, *Can I be revived if I meet the conditions?* The answer is yes. "Revival," it has been said, "is God's finger pointed at you." The present powerlessness of the church may be a sign that God has withdrawn His blessing that we might seek Him. Our desperation is a sign of hope.

We must create a climate in which the Holy Spirit is so free to work that channels are readied for whatever God chooses to do. We should not be idle, simply "waiting for the fire to fall." Whether America has another chance is up to God; whether we are faithful is up to us.

Since the harvest we reap is largely dependent upon the seeds we plant, it is clear that we must sow the seed of the gospel well watered with prayer. Let us never doubt that God can shake a church and its community with His presence so that men and women seek God for forgiveness and cleansing. *What God has done in the past, He can do again!*

Revival can never be engineered by a committee or a team of preachers. God must take the initiative; even our cry to Him for mercy is prompted by His work in our hearts. Repentance is a gift of His grace.

What can we do as the Holy Spirit works in our hearts?

1. *We must support those national prayer movements* that are even now having a profound impact on our churches. Concerts of prayer are springing up everywhere. Prayer summits for pastors began in the Northwest and are now taking place in many major cities.

Prayer movements that unite denominations under the banner of the gospel must be organized. As Jonathan Edwards taught, united prayer is more powerful than the accumulated prayers of individuals. The vision of revival must be kept before us.

God may be calling one of us to be the next Jeremiah Lanphier, a man with a vision to mobilize people to pray. Let us take God's admonition to five of the seven churches of Revelation, and "Repent."

2. *We must learn the principles of faith and boldness* that will prepare us to survive a crisis. Revival in America has often been stimulated through some national calamity — economic reversals, for instance. Obviously none of us hopes for the unravelling of our economy, but this just might be the catalyst that will call this nation back to God. If this happens, let us be ready to point the way.

3. *We must individually stand for Christ* in the courts, in the schools, in politics and business. This is not the time to surrender, hoping for a miracle that will exempt us from the persecution others have endured. We cannot ignore our flight from the inner cities of our nation; we cannot condone our fear in the face of the world's intimidation. Witnessing must be our priority.

4. *We must renew our interest in the history of revival*; such studies stimulate faith and prayer. Unbelief — the idea that we have drifted too far for God to do anything

— often stands in the way of the display of His power. Christ could do no great works in Nazareth because of unbelief (Matthew 13:58).

We've learned that news of revival spreads revival. If a revival were to begin in the United States, thousands of Christians would want to become a part of the miracle.

5. *We must pursue holy living no matter the cost.* Some have already caught the vision of what Christ can do and proved it in their own lives. We must separate ourselves from the world's values, leisure, and compromises. The church must maintain purity.

Presently in America there are many tributaries that might converge into a river of spiritual blessing. Our responsibility is to make sure that our part of the land is watered. That can happen only if we stay on our knees until we believe that the gospel truly saves.

Billy Sunday aptly wrote, "One spark of fire can do more to prove the power of gunpowder than a whole library written on the subject." Revived Christians beget revival. It must begin with us, in our own homes where our true character is revealed and in our churches where our burning hearts can ignite others.

In 1635 B.C. an Arab chief nicknamed "Faras the horseman" was traveling through the desert with a large herd of horses. Suddenly far in the distance a body of water came into view. The herd, crazed by thirst, broke into a stampede, racing toward the stream. Farras tested the obedience of the animals by blowing loudly on his horn, sounding the call to battle. Out of that great herd, five horses stopped in their tracks, wheeled around, and returned to obey the call. These five mares, the story goes, became the stock of the world-famous Arabian horses.

Our nation is dashing madly toward a distant mirage. Even some within the church have joined the quest to find fulfillment somewhere, other than in God. The Almighty has sounded the alarm for battle; He looks for a few to return and stand for Him at great personal cost at this time of national crisis. Perhaps He will take a few earnest souls and use them to begin a national awakening.

Will America be given another chance? Let's change the question: *Has the church been given another chance?* A chance to repent, to evangelize, and to win battles that might bring this nation back from the ditch into which we have slid? Here is where we begin:

45

Submit therefore to God. Resist the devil and he will flee from you. Draw near to God and He will draw near to you. Cleanse your hands ye sinners and purify your hearts, you double-minded. Be miserable and mourn and weep; let your laughter be turned into mourning, and your joy to gloom. Humble yourselves in the presence of the Lord, and He will exalt you. (James 4:7-10)

Only by such obedience can we be ready for whatever God has planned for our nation. Thankfully, ours is the God of "another chance."

For a full-length discussion of the issues facing our nation, see *Twelve Myths Americans Believe* by Erwin W. Lutzer (Chicago: Moody, 1993).

Other booklets by Erwin W. Lutzer:

Moody Press, a ministry of the Moody Bible Institute, is designed for education, evangelization, and edification. If we may assist you in knowing more about Christ and the Christian life, please write us without obligation: Moody Press, c/o MLM, Chicago, Illinois 60610.